Making a Cake

Carmel Reilly

NELSON
A Cengage Company

Australia • Brazil • Japan • Korea • Mexico • Singapore • Spain • United Kingdom • United States

Making a Cake

Fast Forward
Yellow Level 8

Text: Carmel Reilly
Editor: Johanna Rohan
Design: Vonda Pestana
Series design: James Lowe
Production controller: Hanako Smith
Photo research: Corrina Tauschke
Audio recordings: Juliet Hill, Picture Start
Spoken by: Matthew King and Abbe Holmes
Reprint: Jennifer Foo

Acknowledgements
The author and publisher would like to acknowledge permission to reproduce material from the following sources: APL/Corbis/Gabe Palmer, p 12; Istockphoto.com/Matt Billings, p. 9/ Arlene Gee, p. 14 bottom/ Greg Nicholas, p. 11/ Duncan Walker, p. 3 centre; Photo Edit/ David Young-Wolff, pp. 6, 13 top; Photolibrary.com/Foodpix, pp. 4, 7, 10, 13 bottom right; Picture Arts/Steve Cohen, p. 14 top/ Alexandra Grablewski, p. 15 bottom/ Steven Mark Needham, p. 10 top left/ Alison Miksch, p. 8/ Ann Stratton, cover, 1; Smart Digital, p. 15 top.

ISBN 978 0 17 012523 9
ISBN 978 0 17 012513 0 (set)

Cengage Learning Australia
Level 7, 80 Dorcas Street
South Melbourne, Victoria Australia 3205
Phone: 1300 790 853

Cengage Learning New Zealand
Unit 4B Rosedale Office Park
331 Rosedale Road, Albany, North Shore NZ 0632
Phone: 0800 449 725

For learning solutions, visit **cengage.com.au**

Printed in Australia by Ligare Pty Ltd
7 8 9 10 11 12 13 22 21 20 19 18

Evaluated in independent research by staff from the Department of Language, Literacy and Arts Education at the University of Melbourne.

Contents

Chapter 1

Art or Science?

Is making a cake like making a work of **art**? Or is making a cake **science**?

Some people think making a cake is art. They say it is all about how good the cake looks and tastes.

But some people think that making a cake is science. They say it is all about the changes that happen when many **ingredients** are **mixed** together to make something new.

Chapter 2

Art

A lot of work goes into making a cake a work of art.
The person who makes the cake
has to have the right ingredients
to make the cake taste good.
The ingredients have to be mixed in the right way
and cooked at the right temperature.
These things make the cake look and taste good.

Running Words 124

After the cake is cooked, it can be iced.
This also makes a cake look and taste good.

Chapter 3

Science

Cooking a cake is a good way to look at chemical change. Chemical changes happen when you mix different ingredients together to make something new.

Sometimes, the changes happen when the ingredients are heated.

A chemical change is when things have been changed and cannot be changed back.

Melting chocolate
to make icing for a cake is
a physical change.

First, the chocolate is hard.
Then the chocolate is heated.
The heat melts the chocolate, and it goes runny.
When the runny chocolate goes on the cake,
it cools down and goes back
to hard chocolate again.

Physical change is when the thing that has been changed can be changed back.

Chapter 4

Changes

Some people say that making a cake is not always art.
Cakes do not always look and taste good.
The cake will come out flat, hard or lumpy
if the right ingredients are not mixed
and cooked in the right way.

Some people say that
making a cake is always science.
There is always a change when
the ingredients are mixed and heated,
even if the ingredients
are not mixed together well.

The best cakes are part science and part art. It is the chemical and physical changes that make the ingredients into a cake.

But it is the art of the cook
that makes the cake
look and taste good.

Glossary

art the creation of works such as painting or sculpture

ingredients foods that are combined to make something else – e.g. a cake

mixed to be combined together

science the study of the structure and behaviour of things in the world

Index